# HISTORIC
# St. Augustine

# HISTORIC
# St. Augustine

DILLON PRESS
Parsippany, New Jersey

by Sandra Steen and Susan Steen

## Photo Credits:

Front Cover: St. Augustine Historical Society.
Back Cover: Sandra Steen.

Kenneth M. Barrett. Jr.: 26, 53.  Florida State Archives: 9, 11, 14, 24, 50.
Historic Florida Militia: 18, 22.  Sandra Steen/Historic St. Augustine
Preservation Board: 33, 37, 38, 39.  Ken Laffal: title pages.  St. Augustine
Historical Society: 15, 28, 46, 48, 64.  Sandra Steen: 8, 56, 60, 62, 65.

## Library of Congress Cataloging-in-Publication Data

Steen, Sandra.
    Historic St. Augustine / by Sandra Steen and Susan Steen. — 1st ed.
    p. cm. — (Places in American history)
  Includes index.
  Summary:  Looks at St. Augustine, Florida, the oldest continuously
  inhabited European settlement in the United States, from its early days
  to the present.
  ISBN 0-382-39332-5 (LSB). — ISBN 0-382-39331-7 (pbk.)
  1. Saint Augustine (Fla.)—History—Juvenile literature. [1. Saint
  Augustine (Fla.)—History.] I. Steen, Susan. II. Title. III. Series.
  F319.S2S74 1997
  975.9'18—dc20        96-10619

Cover and book design by Lisa Ann Arcuri

 Published by Dillon Press
A Division of Simon & Schuster
299 Jefferson Road, Parsippany, NJ 07054

First Edition

Printed in the United States of America

10 9 8 7 6 5 4 3 2 1

# Contents

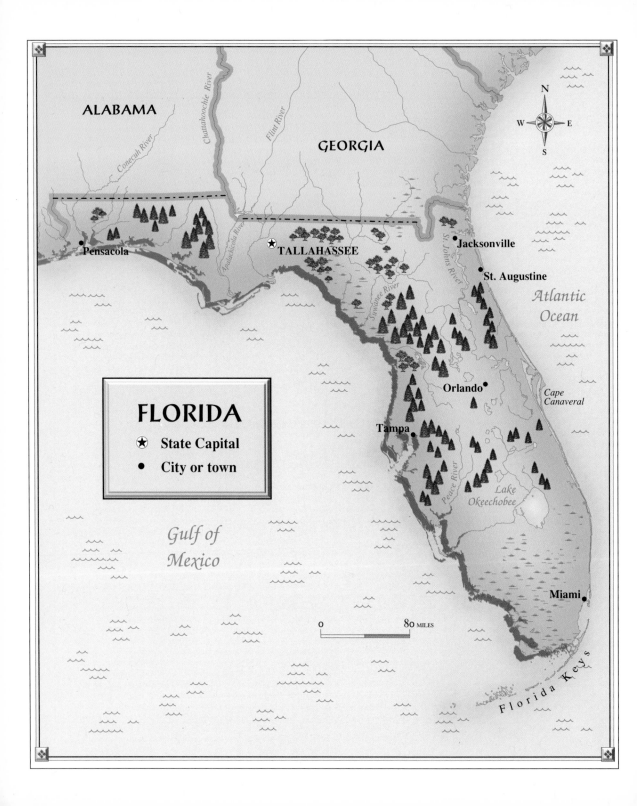

ALABAMA

GEORGIA

*Chuttahoochie River*

*Conecuh River*

*Flint River*

N
W · E
S

Atlantic
Ocean

•Pensacola

*Apalachicola River*

★ TALLAHASSEE

•Jacksonville

•St. Augustine

*Suwanee River*

*St. Johns River*

Orlando•

Cape
Canaveral

Tampa•

*Peace River*

Lake
Okeechobee

FLORIDA

★ State Capital

• City or town

Gulf of
Mexico

Miami•

0        80 MILES

F l o r i d a   K e y s

# CHAPTER 1

# Spanish Explorers

The sailor on lookout aboard the Spanish ship *Santa Maria de Consolación* shouted, "Tierra!" (Land!)

On deck, Juan Ponce de León, a Spanish explorer who had sailed with Christopher Columbus in 1493, also sighted the land. He surveyed the dangerous reefs looming ahead and then signaled his other two ships not to anchor.

As they sailed north, heavy rain pounded the decks, and waves tossed the ships farther out to sea. After the storm the lookout sighted land again. This time the ships anchored.

Standing on deck on April 3, 1513, Ponce de León marveled at the abundance of flowers, birds, and trees that he saw. He could even smell the fragrance of the distant flowers.

*A cross was laid in 1513 by Juan Ponce de León's men to claim the land for Spain.*

Ponce de León and his crew waded ashore and planted a Spanish flag on the beach. They claimed all the land on the eastern coastline of North America in the name of King Ferdinand of Spain. Since it was Easter season, called *Pascua Florida* in Spanish, Ponce de León named the land *La Florida*, "land of flowers." Historical records confirm that this spot later became the settlement of St. Augustine.

*Juan Ponce de León at the Fountain of Youth*

It is said that Spanish explorers built a cross to claim the land, as was the custom. Ponce de León's men arranged stones in the ground. They placed a row of 15 stones from east to west and a row of 13 stones overlapping the first row to form the cross. The numbers 15 and 13 represented the year of discovery—1513.

While searching for gold, Ponce de León may also have searched for the Fountain of Youth. According to legend, an elderly Native American woman from Puerto Rico told him about an island with magical waters. Those who bathed in the fountain would become young forever. At the time, the story seemed believable to Ponce de León. He had seen Native Americans work "magic" on people, using plants to stop bleeding and reduce fever. Perhaps he thought that the waters would make him young and help his ailing king and that the discovery would secure him a favorable place in history.

Long before explorers came to the New World, the Timucuas lived in eastern Florida. These Native Americans established the village of Seloy, near what is now St. Augustine. They respected their environment.

The men wore little clothing. They covered their bodies with bear grease to keep away fleas and mosquitoes. They knotted their hair on top of their heads, perhaps to dare their enemies to try to scalp them. Sometimes the men wore red-dyed fish bladders tied through their pierced ears.

*The Timucuas cooked their game on a rack over an open fire.*

These air-filled bladders must have looked like small balloons dangling from their ears.

Only the chief's family members tattooed themselves. Using thorns, they drew designs on their bodies and painted them red, blue, and black.

The women pulled Spanish moss from trees and made skirts. They didn't knot their hair but let it hang down their backs. They wore bracelets made of shells, pearls, and shark teeth. Strings of copper ornaments jingled from their hips and waists as they walked. Timucuan women planted corn, gathered bird eggs, and prepared meals. They also made pottery and baskets for storing their food.

The warriors fished, built huts, and made weapons. When they hunted alligators, they rammed pointed logs down the animals' throats. Then they clubbed the animals to death.

The Timucuas stored their food in the Bujio, the chief's hut. The Bujio stood in the center of the village. All community decisions were made there. Many small round huts surrounded the Bujio. A log wall encircled the village for protection.

During battles, Timucuan warriors fought with spears, slings, blowguns, and stone axes. They also shot arrows with tips made from flint or shark teeth. Sometimes they used poisoned tips. After battle, the warriors scalped their enemies. Then they cut off their enemies' arms and legs and displayed them in the village.

Usually the warriors stopped fighting before sunset. Other Timucuas removed their dead from the battlefield and buried them. Then the widows cut their own hair and scattered it over the burial mounds. Timucuan custom forbade these women to remarry until they grew their hair long again.

In September 1565, Admiral Pedro Menéndez de Avilés and his men anchored several Spanish ships in the harbor near the Seloy village. King Phillip II of Spain had ordered Menéndez to destroy the nearby French settlement, Fort Caroline, and to colonize Florida for Spain.

Menéndez ordered a scouting party to go ashore. The Timucuan chief offered the Spaniards the use of the Bujio. For better protection from the French, the Spaniards dug a moat, or a ditch, around the Bujio, making it a fort. Because their tools had not arrived, the men dug the moat with their fingernails. Part of this moat has been uncovered by archaeologists.

On September 8, about 500 soldiers, 200 sailors, and 100 settlers assembled ashore. Cannons boomed. Banners waved. People shouted over pounding drums and the blare of trumpets.

*The first Mass conducted in St. Augustine*

Then Father López, a Catholic priest, stepped forward, singing and carrying a cross. Menéndez knelt and kissed the cross. Then Father López conducted the first Mass in St. Augustine. Since Menéndez had spotted land on August 28, the feast day of Saint Augustine, an early Christian, he named the settlement St. Augustine.

Fearing an attack by the French, the Spaniards unloaded their supplies and secured the fort. Meanwhile a fleet of ships carrying 600 French soldiers sailed down the coast toward St. Augustine. Suddenly a hurricane struck, scattering and wrecking their ships.

*A painting of Pedro Menéndez de Avilés, mustering his troops*

With the French stranded, Menéndez realized that Fort Caroline would be defenseless. He marched 500 Spanish soldiers 45 miles north to the French settlement. For days, rain pounded their bodies. Soaked, they struggled through flooded swamps, creeks, and rivers. The downpour muffled their approach to the fort. Then just before dawn, Spanish soldiers surprised the sleeping French. They killed the men but spared the women and children. About 100 French escaped.

Menéndez left several soldiers to guard Fort Caroline. As he and his men headed back to St. Augustine, Menéndez received word that a French troop was marching toward the settlement. By now the Spaniards outnumbered the French. Since the French troops were scattered, the Spanish soldiers captured them, encountering little resistance.

There was not enough food or shelter for the French prisoners and the Spaniards. Menéndez gave the French a choice—either join the Catholic Spanish forces or prepare to die. Since most of these French people were not Catholic, nearly half chose death over becoming Catholic. According to Spanish law at that time, anyone opposed to the Catholic religion would be burned to death. Menéndez ignored the law and had the Frenchmen beheaded instead.

St. Augustine struggled through the first year. The Spanish soldiers refused to farm. Some fished or hunted bear and deer for food. Supply ships often sank. The Timucuas shared their food with the settlers, but hundreds of the Spaniards still deserted or died. However, the birth of the first Spanish child in the colony gave them new hope for the future.

Spanish soldiers treated the Timucuas badly. They ordered them to build houses, roads, and missions, the first being *Nombre de Dios*. The soldiers also forced them to plant wheat, grapes, and orange trees brought from Spain. The priests taught the Timucuas the Catholic religion. After a while the Timucuas refused to work. Angered, Menéndez ordered two chiefs to be whipped in public.

During the next few years, tensions between Timucuas and Spaniards increased. Some Spaniards married Timucuan women. Many Timucuas died from diseases brought from Spain. Other Timucuas rebelled against the Spaniards and Christianity and burned down the missions.

Finally the Spaniards moved their settlement a short distance south. They built a small wooden fort that served as a military outpost. More settlers deserted; others died. By 1572 the survivors depended upon the 12 remaining farmers for food.

Native Americans, as well as pirates, continued to attack the weak settlement. In 1586, Sir Francis Drake, an English navigator and admiral

*A reenactment of the looting of St. Augustine in 1586 by Sir Francis Drake and his men*

with orders from Queen Elizabeth I of England, swooped down on St. Augustine. His fleet of 42 ships and 2,000 soldiers outnumbered the Spanish colonists. The Spaniards fired a few cannonballs before fleeing into the forest. Then Drake and his men looted St. Augustine and burned it to the ground.

**CHAPTER 2**

# Castillo de San Marcos

**A**fter St. Augustine burned in 1586, Spanish settlers rebuilt their town. Six years later, Franciscan friars, Catholic missionaries, arrived from Spain. They taught Native Americans how to improve farming and raise cattle. The friars and the Native Americans built mission walls from wood or "wattle and daub." First they interwove poles and branches to form a wall, and then they covered it with clay. The friars also taught Native Americans to read and write and to sing and play music.

At the turn of the century, hurricanes flooded St. Augustine, leaving the settlers homeless. Termites, fires, and the rotting of wooden buildings also destroyed the town. After each disaster the settlers rebuilt their homes and fort.

By 1620, St. Augustine, now 55 years old, had more than 100 homes and shops, a fish market, a church, and a six-bed hospital. In the same year, Jamestown, Virginia, was a 13-year-old English settlement with its own government. Also in 1620 the *Mayflower*, carrying 102 Pilgrims, landed at Plymouth, Massachusetts, to form a colony.

Through the years the fort at St. Augustine had served as a military outpost for the Spanish territories Florida and *Nueva España* (Mexico). Spanish trading ships used the constantly moving Gulf Stream, a warm ocean current near Florida. The king of Spain ordered his soldiers to provide safe passage of these ships to and from Mexico and Spain. In addition, he ordered Mexico to pay a yearly sum to St. Augustine for this protection. The colonists and soldiers needed this money to buy food, clothes, gunpowder, and other supplies that were shipped from Spain and Mexico. The money usually arrived late or not at all.

One spring day in 1668, John Davis, also known as Robert Searles, an English pirate, captured a Spanish ship off the shores of St. Augustine. On board, Dr. Pedro Piques, a French surgeon, complained to Davis about St. Augustine's governor, who had slapped his face and fired him over a personal matter. The men exchanged information about the riches that passed through the port. When Davis learned that the fort was poorly protected, he and the doctor plotted an attack on St. Augustine.

On May 28, Davis anchored the captured ship in St. Augustine's harbor. Because the townspeople were expecting a shipment of flour and the troops' payroll, they didn't suspect a thing.

Around midnight approximately 100 pirates lowered boats from the ship and rowed toward land. When Davis spotted a fisherman swiftly paddling his canoe to shore, he raised his pistol. Two shots rang out. The wounded fisherman's screams alerted the guards.

Davis and his men scrambled ashore. Some pirates ran to the fort's guardhouse. Others invaded houses—shooting, killing, and looting.

*A reenactment of the attack on St. Augustine by John Davis and his band of pirates*

Davis and a few men tried to take the fort. They failed because most of the other pirates were hauling treasures back to their ship. During the raid the colonists killed 11 pirates and wounded 19, but in the end, the pirates had murdered 60 colonists.

When Davis returned to his ship, he found it crammed with treasures and 70 prisoners. Angry, Davis traded the prisoners for meat, firewood, and water. Longing for a new adventure and more treasures, he ordered the pirates to set sail. Dr. Piques was left behind.

News of pirate raids and of the English settling in nearby Spanish territory reached Spain. King Carlos II, fearing a loss of wealth and power in the New World, ordered the

construction of a permanent stone fort. St.
Augustine's settlers had already rebuilt the
wooden fort nine times. By the summer of 1671,
the governor of St. Augustine had hired skilled
workers and an engineer from nearby Habana
(Havana), Cuba. Soon money, supplies, and
soldiers arrived from Spain.

Shortly after, stonecutters chopped blocks of
shellstone, called coquina, out of pits from nearby
Anastasia Island. Workers loaded the large
blocks onto wagons. Oxen pulled the wagons to
the wharf. There Native Americans, slaves, and
convicts hauled the blocks onto rafts that ferried
them across the river to the building site.

Meanwhile other workers dumped oyster shells
into hot kilns, or ovens. The heated shells changed
into lime, which was used for mortar to hold the
coquina blocks together for the fort's walls.

On Sunday, October 2, 1672, at four o'clock in
the afternoon, workers and officials gathered for the
ground breaking of the new fort, Castillo de San
Marcos. Governor Cendoya thrust a spade into the

*In this drawing, Timucuas are shown building the Castillo de San Marcos.*

ground and dug the first hole for the foundation trench. Laborers continued to haul stones and dig trenches. A month later the governor laid the first foundation stone. Construction of the fort took about 23 years and cost more than 138,375 pesos, about $220,000, using the labor of hundreds of workers.

The Castillo walls stood 33 feet above the moat. The north, south, and west walls ranged in thickness from 14 feet at the base to 9 feet at the top. The east wall, facing the bay, ranged in thickness from 19 feet at the base to 11 feet at the top.

The four walls formed a square with diamond-shaped corners jutting out. These bastions served as defense lookouts. Using the best wood from the old fort, carpenters built various rooms to store gunpowder, weapons, food, and supplies. Soldiers used the other rooms as temporary living quarters, a guardhouse, and a chapel.

A moat 40 feet wide and 8 feet deep surrounded the Castillo. Two drawbridges provided protection from invasions. One connected the fort's gate to the ravelin, a small building on the south side of

*The moat and towers of the massive fort Castillo de San Marcos helped it withstand many assaults.*

the Castillo. A smaller drawbridge connected the ravelin to land. This was the only way in or out. Soldiers raised the drawbridges every night.

Native Americans earned one "real" a day, or about $.20, plus two to three pounds of maize (corn) flour. Unskilled workers made four reales, or $.80, a day. Skilled workers and craftsmen received 10–20 reales, up to $4.00, a day. The Castillo engineer earned the most—three pesos a day, or about $4.75.

To keep construction moving on schedule, 150 workers were needed. However, only about 100 diggers, haulers, and mortar mixers worked at one time. Because of the labor shortage, Governor Cendoya recruited convicts and slaves, who earned no pay for their work. Instead these men received servings of meat, fish, and maize flour.

Over the years, yellow fever, smallpox, and lack of funds slowed the construction of the Castillo. In the 1680s, workers fell behind schedule. The governor begged and received permission from the church to work on Sundays and holidays. After one English attack, nearly every able-bodied person, including women, worked day and night on the Castillo. To show the progress of the Castillo, the governor sent a wooden model to the king.

To keep soldiers and workers from starving, farmers planted maize in the clearing around the fort. Soon rows of corn provided plenty of food. But

*An interior view of Castillo de San Marcos*

when the king heard about this, he ordered that
the fields be destroyed. He feared that the enemy
could easily hide between the tall cornstalks.

Before the Castillo's completion in 1695,
English soldiers and pirates continued to invade
St. Augustine. In 1702, after destroying some
nearby missions, Governor James Moore of the
Carolina colony and 800 soldiers marched into
town. At the same time, a fleet of English ships

arrived in the harbor. Under the protection of 230 Spanish soldiers, 1,500 men, women, and children raced inside the Castillo.

The attackers captured St. Augustine and surrounded the fort. To prevent the invaders from using the empty houses for cover, Spanish soldiers fired upon and destroyed many houses near the fort. They fought the English for nearly two months. Fortunately Spanish warships arrived and blocked the English ships in the harbor. Trapped, Governor Moore ordered his men to burn his ships. As the English soldiers fled on foot, they set fire to the town. Later Moore and his men returned to Florida and destroyed what was left of the Franciscan mission system.

Even though the fort had withstood the attacks, the town and the Franciscan monastery, with its priceless library, were burned down. Once again the residents rebuilt St. Augustine.

# CHAPTER 3

# Colonial St. Augustine

In 1731, Spanish coast guards caught Robert Jenkins, a British captain, trading with Spanish colonists. The Spanish government allowed only Spanish ships to trade with Spanish colonists. The coast guards considered Jenkins's trading an act of smuggling. According to Jenkins, a Spanish officer cut off his ear as punishment. The officer handed Jenkins the ear and threatened to do the same to the king of England. Back in London, Jenkins showed his severed ear to members of the British government.

After years of disagreements about trade routes and land in North America, the British government declared war on Spain. The war, which became known as the War of Jenkins's

Ear, began in 1740. Governor James Oglethorpe of the Georgia colony led an army of 1,400 British soldiers and Native Americans in an attack on St. Augustine. The attackers anchored their seven warships offshore and bombarded the Castillo. The cannonballs bounced off the coquina walls, barely making dents. For 27 days the British blasted the fort but failed to capture it.

Oglethorpe planned another attack on the fort, but his troops refused to fight. They feared the dangers of the approaching hurricane season. On the 38th day of siege, the British left. Weary and starving, the colonists returned to their homes.

During the 1740s about 2,000 Spanish people lived in St. Augustine. The families of the soldiers usually lived in one-story, coquina-walled houses. They plastered the walls and painted them white. Sometimes they painted the walls red or a yellowish orange. Closed wooden shutters kept out the cold in winter. Since there were no fireplaces with chimneys, family members kept warm by sitting near a *brasero*, a metal pan

filled with hot coals. In the summer, smoke from
the brasero kept away mosquitoes.

These 18th-century houses usually had two
rooms. Most families had a shrine of a favorite
saint on the wall for worship. They furnished
their houses with chests for clothes, tables,
chairs, and bedrolls. At night they used chamber
pots as toilets. In the morning a family member
or slave threw the waste into the bay.

Spanish women planted gardens of corn,
cabbages, squash, sweet potatoes, peppers, toma-
toes, and herbs. They also cultivated beans,
grapes, onions, and pumpkins. Citrus and fig
trees grew in the yards. Most families raised
chickens and pigs for food.

The men fished for mullet and catfish in
nearby rivers. They gathered clams and oysters.
Sometimes they traded with Native Americans
for wild animals, birds, and fish. Or they hunted
for themselves.

The women often cooked meals in outdoor
kitchens made from poles and a palm-frond

*Meals were cooked in outdoor kitchens with thatched roofs.*

thatched roof. They filled a cast-iron kettle with fresh foods. The meals simmered over an open fire. At noon the family gathered for the main meal. They ate from homemade wooden bowls and spoons or Mexican or Native American pottery.

In order to get water for drinking and cooking, men dug their own wells. They bought wooden barrels, available from the supply ships, and removed the ends. Then they shoved three or four barrels down the hole to make a shaft for the well. Every day they lowered a bucket to get fresh water. People rarely bathed because they thought it was unhealthy.

Soldiers earned low wages, so families learned not to be wasteful. Only broken and useless items went into the garbage. People burned oyster shells to make lime. Then they mixed sand and water with the lime to patch their walls. People even saved cow bones to make handles for their tools and buttons for their clothes.

Children worked more than they played. They helped care for the gardens and animals, prepare food, and clean up. When the children finished their chores, they liked to play marbles or a kind of checkers called "fox and geese." Sometimes they rolled barrel hoops down the sandy streets, stopping runaway hoops with sticks.

Most children in St. Augustine did not get an education. Very few adults knew how to read or were able to teach the children. In 1740 about 22 soldiers out of 100 could read and 12 could write. At age ten, boys learned a trade by becoming apprentices. Some boys worked with cabinetmakers, and others with blacksmiths. At age 15 most boys joined the

Spanish army or militia. Many girls married at 13 and started families.

Colonial women wore a skirt, a bodice, a vest, and an apron. The bodice, a long blouse that hung below the knees, could be worn as a day dress or nightgown. They wore the vest and skirt over the bodice. Women used their aprons to carry such things as vegetables and twigs. When working, they spread the apron around the skirt to keep the skirt clean. Otherwise, they wore the apron bunched up in front. A scarf tied around their head protected their hair and kept it clean. Women rarely shampooed their hair.

Women bought cloth shipped from England. They cut the cloth and hand sewed it into clothes. They did not bother to measure for size because one size fit all. If a garment was too large, its owner gathered up the extra cloth and tied it or rolled it up. Since cloth was so expensive, most people in St. Augustine owned only one or two sets of clothes.

Sometimes women carried a woolen cloth pocket, a pouch tied on a band and worn around the waist. They slid the pocket through a slit in the side of their skirts to hide it. The pocket held all kinds of things, including valuables. Women embroidered or sewed designs on their pockets. In addition to sewing, women knitted socks for the soldiers and shawls for themselves.

Three blacksmiths owned shops in St. Augustine. These shops, similar to today's hardware stores, sold nails, kettle hooks, hinges, and chains. The blacksmith also made latches, locks, and tools, such as rakes, hoes, and axes.

Each morning the blacksmith tossed charcoal into the forge, or furnace. Next he pumped two large leather bellows, which blew air into the fire. With a pair of tongs, the blacksmith held a strip of iron in the fire. When the end of the strip turned red hot, he set it on the anvil, a large block of iron with a flat top.

With his other hand, he picked up a hammer to shape the hot, soft iron. *Tap-tap. Tap-tap.* The

*The blacksmith made all kinds of essential hardware and tools.*

blacksmith hammered the iron strip into a kettle hook. He snapped off the hook that was still hot and dipped it into water. *Hisssss!* The hook cooled and hardened. The blacksmith hung the new hook on the wall to sell.

At noon the blacksmith cooked his meal over the forge. Most of his food came from the small garden outside his shop. At night the blacksmith climbed up to the loft above his shop and went to sleep.

Another craftsman, the cabinetmaker, also lived in his shop. He built tables, chairs, benches,

*The cabinetmaker built and repaired furniture with simple hand tools.*

and cabinets. For part of the day he repaired broken furniture brought in by townspeople. If people wanted a decorated piece of furniture, they had to order it from Cuba or Spain.

The cabinetmaker chose wood from the many kinds of hardwood trees that grew near St. Augustine. He used simple hand tools. To sand wood, he rubbed a piece of broken glass across it. Glass rubbing gave a better finish than today's sandpaper.

The shopkeeper sold goods that families could not easily produce at home. He stocked oil, wine, tobacco, pipes, molasses, grains, gunpowder,

*Shopkeepers chained mugs to barrels to prevent customers from taking them.*

and much more. Most of these goods were made in Europe or Mexico. Besides buying goods, townspeople often stopped at the shop to hear the latest news. While they talked, the men drank rum from mugs. The shopkeeper chained the mugs to the rum barrels so that customers wouldn't walk off with them.

Shopkeepers bought European goods from privateers, who were sea captains licensed by the Spanish government. The Spanish government allowed privateers to capture enemy ships and seize the goods or booty. The king of Spain and the governor of St. Augustine received a percentage of the booty. Shopkeepers sometimes purchased these goods from smugglers and pirates.

For more than 200 years, Spain controlled St. Augustine. Then around 1760, the Spanish sided with the French during the French and Indian War, known in Europe as the Seven Years' War. In this war the British fought the French and Native Americans for control of North America. When the British captured Cuba, an island south of Florida, Spain entered the war.

Spain and France lost the war. A peace agreement, called the Treaty of Paris, gave Florida to Great Britain and Cuba back to Spain. In 1763 the British took control of Castillo de San Marcos, St. Augustine, and Florida, ending 250 years of Spanish occupation.

# CHAPTER 4

# From British to Spanish to American

In 1763 about 3,000 Spaniards who chose not to live under British rule loaded their belongings and set sail for Cuba. Then British ships arrived at St. Augustine with military reinforcements, new colonists, government officials, and supplies.

British soldiers marched into town, broke into abandoned houses, and searched for anything of value. They tore down fences for firewood. Later some British residents repaired the houses and added fireplaces, chimneys, and glass windows.

The British government divided the Florida territory into two separate colonies and chose St. Augustine as the capital of East Florida. For additional space they added wooden second floors to some of the rooms at the Castillo, which they called

Fort St. Mark. The government hired a schoolmaster and constructed the King's Road, a 16-foot-wide road connecting St. Augustine to Georgia.

Years later during the American Revolution, when the British fought against the colonists, the fort held many kinds of prisoners. Three South Carolina signers of the Declaration of Independence—Thomas Heyward, Arthur Middleton, and Edward Rutledge—spent time in a jail cell in the fort.

The British army recruited Seminoles and Creeks. They also enlisted trusted black slaves to bear arms. Many blacks intermarried with the Seminoles. Soldiers set up regulations to distinguish free blacks from slaves. A free black wore a silver armband with the word *free* engraved on it. A slave wore a heart-shaped badge.

Free blacks and slaves sold vegetables, fish, cakes, and beer at the public market on the plaza. If they were caught selling outside the market, soldiers whipped the offenders 39 times. They also whipped any blacks caught dancing after ten o'clock at night.

When the British lost the war, the 1783 treaty demanded the return of Florida to Spain. Fewer than 50 Spaniards returned to St. Augustine from Cuba. When the British left, they removed some of the wooden houses and loaded them on ships. The new government refused to pay for the British church bell and the fire engine. The British then shipped them to their new residence, the nearby British Bahama islands.

In the early 1800s Spanish colonies in Central and South America and Mexico fought for freedom from Spain. The wars with the colonies along with problems at home caused Spain to lose money and power. Finally, Spain formally deeded the Florida territory to the United States in 1821. The United States paid about $5 million to American settlers to settle claims for property damage but nothing to Spain directly.

The Americans honored General Francis Marion, a hero of the American Revolution. They changed the name of Castillo de San Marcos to Fort Marion because of his leadership and achievements.

In the 1820s, plantation owners profited from exporting sugar and millions of oranges. By the mid-1830s, frost destroyed the sugar cane and oranges. Some orange trees survived only to be eaten by insects. Because of the poor economy, banks refused to lend money to plantation owners to start over.

During the 1830s Dr. Andrew Anderson started silkworm production with 4,000 mulberry trees. Silkworms ate the mulberry leaves and spun silk which was made into cloth. After about ten years the silkworm industry failed because of the overproduction of mulberry trees, which numbered 100,000.

During this time many Americans in Florida claimed Native American land. But the Florida Seminoles fought to keep their land, which was some of Florida's richest farmland. In 1834, General Wiley Thompson presented a treaty to the Seminole nation. The treaty promised them money, supplies, and farmland in the West. The treaty also stated that black Seminoles would be sold as slaves and not sent to the West.

After four chiefs had refused to sign the treaty, Osceola, a Seminole leader, stepped forward. He thrust his knife into the treaty paper. Soldiers then threw Osceola in prison.

Later Osceola only signed the treaty in order to be released from prison. He warned other Seminoles not to side with the Americans. If a Seminole became a traitor, Osceola had him killed.

One day while Osceola was talking to General Thompson at a trading post, slave catchers grabbed Osceola's second wife, a black Seminole. They planned to sell her as a slave. Osceola flew into a rage. Several soldiers held him down and then threw him in jail. Osceola begged General Thompson to return his wife, but Thompson refused.

Thompson realized locking up Osceola was a mistake. He released him. As Osceola rode off to join his wife, he screamed the Seminole war cry, *"Yo-ho-e-he!"* For days, Osceola stalked General Thompson. When the General was left unprotected, Osceola killed him.

*A portrait of Osceola, Seminole leader*

The Seminoles prepared for battle. The American army sent majors and generals to stop Osceola, but he outsmarted them. The soldiers attempted to weaken the Seminoles by stealing their cattle and destroying their food supply. Even when the Seminoles suffered from starvation, they refused to surrender.

The Seminoles fled to the swamps. When soldiers approached, the women placed their children in pits and covered them with palm leaves. Then they hid in the water. The women covered their faces with lily pads, not moving until the enemy left.

President Jackson sent a new general to stop the Seminoles. This general brought bloodhounds to track them. Still the Seminoles stayed out of reach of the soldiers.

Many American soldiers and Seminoles died from malaria, a disease transmitted by mosquito bites. Osceola caught the fever. Weak and starving, he wanted to end the war.

A new treaty promised more money and transportation of black Seminoles to the West. The slave catchers protested. During peace-treaty negotiations, slave catchers continued to seize black Seminoles. Those Seminoles who could, fled.

On October 21, 1837, Osceola arrived near St. Augustine in full ceremonial dress. He carried an egret plume, a sign of peace. A white flag of truce

*A painting of the capture of Osceola*

flew overhead. Osceola met with American officials to talk peace.

The Americans broke their promise. They
wanted to keep all black Seminoles as slaves.
When Osceola refused to give them up, the soldiers
captured Osceola and his men. They were imprisoned at Fort Marion (Castillo de San Marcos).
Some Seminoles escaped and led more uprisings.

For security reasons, soldiers moved Osceola to
Fort Moultrie in South Carolina. Many curious

people visited the Seminole patriot. On January 30, 1838, Osceola died at the age of 34. Soldiers buried him near the fort. The Seminoles never surrendered.

In 1845, Florida became the twenty-seventh state. Then in 1861 the Civil War began. The Northern states, which wanted to end slavery, fought the Southern states, which wanted to keep slavery. Florida sided with the South and seceded (withdrew) from the Union, another name for the United States. The Union troops stationed at Fort Marion never fought in the war. The Civil War finally ended in 1865. The South lost, and Florida was readmitted to the Union in 1868.

In the 1870s many visitors traveled from the North to St. Augustine to escape the cold winters. People with tuberculosis, a lung disease, discovered that the warm climate improved their health.

In 1883, one tourist, Henry Flagler, cofounder of Standard Oil, visited St. Augustine. He thought this beautiful oceanside town could become a resort for wealthy people. He built two grand hotels, Hotel Ponce de León and Hotel Alcazar. Wealthy

*Henry Flagler made many contributions to St. Augustine and to Florida.*

tourists enjoyed dances on top of the Castillo, carriage parades on the beach, and entertainment in the hotels and the plaza.

Since transportation was poor, Flagler bought, improved, and expanded the local railroad line.

Now tourists could come directly from New York to St. Augustine. They purchased land and built houses. Flagler introduced electricity and plumbing to the area. He built houses for his employees and one for his own family.

For a boy who left home at 14 with only a French coin, a nickel, and four pennies in his pocket, Flager made great contributions to St. Augustine and Florida. He kept the French coin to remember what it was like to be poor. Flagler died at age 83 and was buried in the family tomb at Memorial Presbyterian Church.

In 1924, President Coolidge declared Fort Marion a national monument. Later, in 1935, the National Park Service began restoration of the fort. Then in 1942, Congress changed the fort's name back to Castillo de San Marcos. In April of that year, during World War II, German submarines appeared near St. Augustine. German spies watched through binoculars as cars drove along the beach. Later the spies sank U.S. freighters along the Florida coast.

In 1959 the Florida legislature established the St. Augustine Historical Restoration and Preservation Commission. Since then the Commission has acquired, restored, and rebuilt about 23 historical buildings. To obtain accurate information for the restorations, the Commission hired historians, who researched old documents, maps, and drawings from Spain and Florida.

Workers accurately restored or reconstructed buildings, patios, and gardens much as they were in the mid-1700s. Experts made reproductions or bought original furnishings, including lanterns from Spain. One house acquired a 200-year-old crib.

The Spanish government and private U.S. citizens donated time and money to the project. The Commission acquired the Post Office building. The Post Office contained some of the walls from the Colonial Government House, which once stood on this site. Today the Government House serves as a museum.

In May 1964, Martin Luther King, Jr., marched in St. Augustine's plaza. He spoke about

*To celebrate the 500th anniversary of Columbus's arrival in the New World, citizens and visitors observed replicas of his ships in St. Augustine.*

the problems of segregation, the practice of forcing black people to live in separate areas from white people. Dr. King said, "The oldest city was the oldest segregated city in America." On June 12, police arrested Dr. King for protesting.

In 1992, visitors and local citizens of St. Augustine celebrated the 500th anniversary of Columbus's arrival in the New World. They boarded replicas sent from Spain of the *Niña*, the *Pinta*, and the *Santa Maria*.

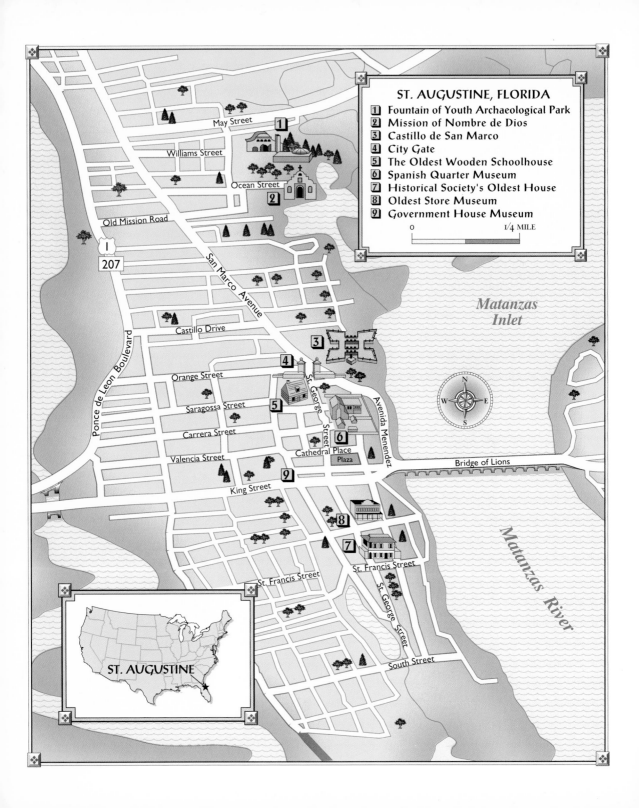

ST. AUGUSTINE, FLORIDA
1 Fountain of Youth Archaeological Park
2 Mission of Nombre de Dios
3 Castillo de San Marco
4 City Gate
5 The Oldest Wooden Schoolhouse
6 Spanish Quarter Museum
7 Historical Society's Oldest House
8 Oldest Store Museum
9 Government House Museum

0                    1/4 MILE

May Street
Williams Street
Ocean Street
Old Mission Road
207
San Marco Avenue
Ponce de Leon Boulevard
Castillo Drive
Orange Street
Saragossa Street
Carrera Street
Valencia Street
St. George Street
Cathedral Place
Plaza
Avenida Menendez
King Street
St. Francis Street
St. Francis Street
St. George Street
South Street

Matanzas Inlet
Matanzas River
Bridge of Lions

N
W      E
S

ST. AUGUSTINE

# Walk Through History

**T**o learn about historic St. Augustine, stop at the Visitors Information Center on Castillo Drive. Admission for children is free, and so are the maps. Watch the film *Discover St. Augustine* for a preview of what you'll see during your visit.

Start where it all began—the Fountain of Youth Archeological Park. You'll see the actual cross Ponce de León laid to claim the land for Spain in 1513. In 1868, property owners covered the cross, but in 1909 a gardener uncovered it. Five years earlier, Dr. Louella Day MacConnell dug up a small silver container at this site. Inside she found a parchment dated 1513 recording the construction of the cross.

As you walk around the park, you'll see skeletons displayed in the burial grounds of Seloy, a

*Enter the City Gate of St. Augustine for a walk through history.*

village of Timucuas. Taste the water from the spring said to be the Fountain of Youth that Ponce de León might have discovered.

Follow your map to the Mission of Nombre de Dios, site of the first mission in the United States. As you walk toward the water, you'll see a 208-foot-high cross. It marks the place where Menéndez landed in 1565 and claimed St. Augustine for Spain. The stainless-steel cross was erected in 1965 to celebrate the 400th anniversary of the founding of St. Augustine.

At the mission each September on Founders Day, men reenact Menéndez's landing. Afterward, local people celebrate Fiesta España in the plaza with Spanish food and entertainment.

Head for the huge Castillo de San Marcos. While crossing the reconstructed bridge, look down into the moat. Long ago when enemies attacked the town, townspeople herded their cows, chickens, and pigs into the dry moat to protect them.

Walk inside the Castillo to the patio, the Plaza de Armas. To your left is a well. At one time three wells provided fresh water for the soldiers. Join National Park rangers as they lead tours. Since a million people visit the Castillo each year, rangers encourage visitors to touch with their eyes instead of their hands.

Explore the rooms surrounding the plaza. Visit the cannonproof storerooms. Here soldiers received food rations, clothes, tools, weapons, and other supplies. As you enter the chapel, you'll see an altar, from which a priest conducted Mass for the soldiers.

When you leave the chapel, turn left to the powder magazine. The thick walls of the vault protected the gunpowder from the enemy, but not from dampness. Once new vaults were built, soldiers moved the gunpowder to drier rooms.

Cross the courtyard to the guardrooms. Guard duty usually lasted 24 hours. During their shifts, soldiers cooked their meals in the large fireplaces and rested on the bunklike beds attached to the walls. Some soldiers passed the time by carving their names in the soft coquina walls. After duty they returned to their homes in town.

Climb the stairs, which were once a ramp, to the gun deck. Small cannons could fire 6-pound balls at a target one mile away. Larger cannons shot 18-pound balls three miles away. From the bell tower the lookout could see three miles away. When he saw an enemy ship, he rang the bell to warn the soldiers and townspeople.

In the 1840s the U.S. Army filled in the moat on the east side of the Castillo. Soldiers mounted weapons along the seawall. They built a furnace to heat cannonballs. When shot at enemy ships, these "red hot" cannonballs set the ships on fire. Check with park rangers for scheduled cannon firings by men in period uniforms.

Some tourists have claimed to see a ghost at the Castillo at sunset. As they walked around the outside, they looked up at the high walls. These tourists described seeing a head with a turban and three feathers hanging down. Some believe it to be the head of Osceola, the Seminole leader, who had been imprisoned in the Castillo. Before Osceola's burial, a doctor had removed his head.

After crossing the street, stop at the City Gate. Long ago, townspeople entered and left their walled city through this gate. In 1808, workers built new twin pillars of white masonry. They covered the roofs of the pillars with red plaster. For the tops they made plaster pomegranates, a kind of red fruit.

As you walk down St. George Street, look to the right at what is claimed to be the oldest wooden schoolhouse in the United States. In the nineteenth century, children attended school here. At first a family lived in this original building. During the Seminole Wars, it served as a guardhouse because of its closeness to the City Gate.

*The oldest wooden schoolhouse in historic St. Augustine*

Carpenters constructed the building with wood from cedar and cypress trees. They hammered the timbers or boards with wooden pegs and hand-made nails. It may seem strange to see a large chain wrapped around the school and fastened to a huge anchor. Some believe that it held the building to the ground during hurricanes.

Inside the classroom lifelike models of students sit at their desks. The student sitting in the corner didn't follow the rules. He wears a dunce cap for punishment. Push the button on the post and listen to the schoolmaster's lesson.

The schoolmaster and his wife lived upstairs. She cooked in the kitchen building, just outside the school. Before you leave, pick up your complimentary diploma.

On the left of St. George Street, tour the restored buildings of the Spanish Quarter Museum. Guides and craftsworkers, dressed in colonial clothing, explain the daily life of the 1740s through the 1840s. You will visit the simple houses of soldiers and a well-to-do family's house. You can smell the wood shavings at the cabinet-maker's shop. Listen and hear hammering at the blacksmith's shop. As you pass an outdoor kitchen, you might smell a stew simmering.

The largest house, the DeMesa-Sánchez House, shows how well-to-do families lived. In the 1840s, visitors sat in the parlor or waiting room until they were invited to the upstairs sitting room.

In the evening, men used the parlor for smoking and conversation. They played games such as cards, dice, chess, and checkers. Look at the large book on the parlor table. It really isn't a book. When opened it became a game board. The game pieces were stored inside. When not in use this "book" stood on a shelf next to real books.

*Chess pieces were hidden in a hollow book to fool the tax collector.*

Women and men followed strict social rules. For example, women couldn't play board games with the men. If a woman gave her opinion while men talked about business or politics, they thought she was slightly insane. She was sent to her room and medicated.

Upstairs, look at the sitting room and bedrooms. House guests often stayed for weeks.

They packed their clothes and valuables in trunks. Men could slide poles through slots in the ends of the trunks and easily carry them anywhere, to travel or if the house caught fire.

Your tour of the Spanish Quarter ends at the Museum Store. Here you may look at or buy various kinds of goods made by craftsworkers.

Next follow your map to 14 St. Francis Street, the location of the Oldest House, also known as the González-Alvarez House. In 1918 the St. Augustine Historical Society acquired the house and, after much research, restored it. The exterior looks new because workers replastered the damaged coquina walls. This house dates back to the early 1700s and represents four periods in history. In the 1600s, thatched wooden houses stood on this site.

A tour guide will show you through the house. The first room represents the Spanish colonial period, when the González family lived here with few furnishings. Don't miss the rat rack hanging from the ceiling. Families stored food there. At

*Notice the rat rack hanging from the ceiling in the Oldest House.*

night when a rat jumped onto the rack, the swaying frightened it away.

When the Peavetts bought the house in 1775, they added a fireplace, front door, glass windows, and a second floor. They changed the downstairs into a tavern, or bar. As you visit the second room, you'll see what a British tavern looked like.

Climb the reconstructed staircase. The second floor displays how the Alvarez family lived during the second Spanish period. The table appears as if the family were about to dine. Since there were no cupboards, families washed the dishes and then set them right back on the table.

*Observe the cannonball in the wall of the Oldest House.*

The Carvers bought the house in 1884. They added a two-story, round tower decorated with conch shells. In the late 1950s, workers removed the crumbling tower.

As you stroll in the courtyard and garden, visit the reconstructed outbuilding or kitchen. Then head for the museum next to the house. Don't miss the cannonball stuck in the coquina wall above the door.

You may want to visit other historic sites in St. Augustine. Stop by the Oldest Store Museum, packed with 100,000 items, from red underwear to a Conestoga wagon. During the 1800s, people even came here to get a haircut or tooth pulled.

Also visit the Government House Museum near the plaza. Exhibits show the history of Native Americans in St. Augustine, European influences, and Flagler's contributions. In one exhibit you'll see gold and silver pieces from Spanish shipwrecks. Archaeological digs on the site continue to add more information from the past.

St. Augustine offers special events throughout the year. At Easter visitors and locals watch the *Parada de los Caballos y Coches*, or "Parade of the Horses and Carriages." Horses wearing decorated hats donated by famous women pull carriages. Marching bands and floats also join the parade.

During the year two important reenactments take place in St. Augustine. In June the Historic Florida Militia act out events of the Spanish Night Watch of the 1740s, when British General Oglethorpe attacked St. Augustine. The members march, wearing Spanish military costumes and carrying torches.

In early December St. Augustine celebrates a British custom called the Grand Illumination.

Men dressed in British colonial costumes reenact the custom of securing the city at sunset. They start at the Government House, carrying torches and keys to the City Gate. Then they parade through the old part of the city accompanied by fife and drum music. The men stop at the City Gate to reenact the locking of the gate. Then they march back to the Government House, cheering the king, and return the keys.

During the summer months, 50 actors present the musical drama *Cross and Sword*, the story of the founding of St. Augustine.

St. Augustine is the oldest, continuously inhabited European settlement in the United States—older than Plimoth Plantation (1620), older than Jamestown (1607). It has survived fires, wars, pirates, hurricanes, yellow fever, four national governments, and tourists. Historic St. Augustine represents the struggle and courage of Native American, African, and European ancestors, especially those of Spanish heritage.

# St. Augustine:
## A HISTORICAL TIME LINE

**1513**   April 3, Juan Ponce de León claims land in the New World for Spain and names it Florida.

**1565**   September, Pedro Menéndez de Avilés claims St. Augustine. Menéndez and his men fight French invaders.

**1586**   Sir Francis Drake loots and burns St. Augustine.

**1668**   John Davis, an English pirate, and his men raid St. Augustine.

**1671**   King Carlos II of Spain orders the construction of a stone fort in St. Augustine.

**1695**   Castillo de San Marcos is completed.

**1702**   English invasion destroys St. Augustine.

**1740**   War of Jenkins's Ear.

**1760**   Spain sides with France in the French and Indian War.

**1763**   Treaty of Paris gives Florida territory to the British.
St. Augustine Spaniards move to Cuba.
British soldiers occupy St. Augustine and rename the Castillo, Fort St. Mark.

**1783**   After the American Revolution, the Treaty of 1783 forces the return of Florida to Spain.

**1787**   The Castillo is renamed Fort Marion.

**1821**   Florida becomes a United States territory.

**1820s**   St. Augustine profits from sugar exports and oranges.

**1830s** Silkworm industry fails.

**1834** Osceola, a Seminole leader, refuses to sign U.S. treaty that forces Seminoles out of Florida.

**1835** Second Seminole War begins.
October 21, U.S. soldiers capture Osceola.

**1838** January 30, Osceola dies of malaria.

**1845** Florida becomes the 27th state.

**1861** Florida secedes from the Union and joins the Confederacy.

**1868** Florida's state government is restored with a new constitution.

**1880s** Henry Flagler builds grand hotels and improves railroad line to St. Augustine.

**1924** Fort Marion becomes a National Monument.

**1935** National Park Service takes control of the fort.

**1942** U.S. Congress changes the fort's name back to Castillo de San Marcos.
April, German submarines appear near beaches of St. Augustine.

**1959** Florida legislature establishes the St. Augustine Historical Restoration and Preservation Commission to restore historic buildings.

**1964** May–June, Martin Luther King, Jr., protests in St. Augustine's plaza and is arrested.
Hurricane Dora hits St. Augustine.

**1965** St. Augustine celebrates its 400th birthday.

**1992** St. Augustine celebrates the 500th anniversary of Columbus's arrival in the New World.

# Visitor Information

## General Information
Most historic sites are within walking distance.

## Visitor Information Center
Open daily from 8:30 A.M. to 5:30 P.M.
Offers maps and pamphlets of historic sites.
Theater shows film *Dream of Empire*. Admission:
$3.00 for adults, $2.00 for children.

## Hours and Admission
*Fountain of Youth:* 9:00 A.M. to 5:00 P.M. daily. Admission:
$4.75 for adults, $1.50 for children.
*Mission of Nombre de Dios:* 7:00 A.M. to 8:00 P.M. in
summer and 9:00 A.M. to 6:00 P.M. in winter.
Donations welcome.
*Castillo de San Marcos:* 9:00 A.M. to 8:00 P.M. in summer
and 8:00 A.M. to 5:15 P.M. in winter. Admission: $2.00.
*Oldest Wooden School House:* 9:00 A.M. to 5:00 P.M. daily.
Admission: $2.00 for adults, $1.00 for children.
*Spanish Quarter Museum:* 9:00 A.M. to 5:00 P.M. daily.
Admission: $10.00 for families, $5.00 for individuals,
$2.50 for children.
*Oldest House:* 9:00 A.M. to 5:00 P.M. daily. Admission:
$5.00 for adults, $3.00 for children.
*Oldest Store Museum:* 9:00 A.M. to 5:00 P.M. daily. Sunday
hours vary. Admission: $4.00 for adults, $1.50 for
children.
*Government House Museum:* 10:00 A.M. to 4:00 P.M.,
Tuesday to Saturday. Closed holidays. Admission:
$2.00 for adults, $1.00 for children.

**Special Events**
*February 15:* Menéndez Day
*Easter Sunday:* St. Augustine Easter Parade
*June:* Drake's Raid reenactment
    Spanish Night Watch at Old Spanish Quarter (two days)
*Summer:* Cannon firings at Castillo de San Marcos
    *Cross and Sword* drama starts at 8:30 P.M. nightly in
    summer except Sunday. Admission: $12:00 for adults,
    $6.00 for children.
*September:* Founders Day/Fiesta España (two days)
*December:* Grand Illumination through old part of the city

**Additional Information**
    Visitor Information Center
    10 Castillo Drive
    St. Augustine, FL 32084
    Phone (904) 824-3334

    St. Augustine/St. Johns County
    Chamber of Commerce
    1 Riberia Street
    St. Augustine, FL 32084
    Phone (904) 829-5681

    Historic St. Augustine Preservation Board
    P.O. Box 1987
    St. Augustine, FL 32085
    Phone (904) 825-5033

# Index